GEARED FOR GROWTH BIBLE STUDIES

PEOPLE AND PROBLEMS
IN THE CHURCH

A STUDY IN 1 CORINTHIANS

BIBLE STUDIES TO IMPACT THE LIVES
OF ORDINARY PEOPLE

Written by Esma Cardinal

The Word Worldwide

CHRISTIAN FOCUS

For details of our titles visit us on our website
www.christianfocus.com

ISBN 1-84550-021-0

Copyright © WEC International

10 9 8 7 6 5 4 3 2 1

Published in 2005 by
Christian Focus Publications Ltd, Geanies House,
Fearn, Tain, Ross-shire, IV20 1TW, Scotland
and
WEC International, Bulstrode, Oxford Road,
Gerrards Cross, Bucks, SL9 8SZ

Cover design by Alister MacInnes

Printed and bound by Bell & Bain, Glasgow

CONTENTS

QUESTIONS AND NOTES

ANSWER GUIDE

PREFACE

GEARED FOR GROWTH

'Where there's LIFE there's GROWTH:
Where there's GROWTH there's LIFE.'

WHY GROW a study group?

Because as we study the Bible and share together we can

* learn to combat loneliness, depression, staleness, frustration, and other problems
* get to understand and love each other
* become responsive to the Holy Spirit's dealing and obedient to God's Word

and that's GROWTH.

How do you GROW a study group?

* Just start by asking a friend to join you and then aim at expanding your group.
* Study the set portions daily (they are brief and easy: no catches).
* Meet once a week to discuss what you find.
* Befriend others, both Christians and non-Christians, and work away together

see how it GROWS!

WHEN you GROW ...

This will happen at school, at home, at work, at play, in your youth group, your student fellowship, women's meetings, mid-week meetings, churches and communities,

you'll be REACHING THROUGH TEACHING.

INTRODUCTORY STUDY

PEOPLE AND PROBLEMS

We are about to study a REAL letter, written by a REAL person (Paul) to REAL people about REAL problems very similar to those we face today. Before we begin our study let's learn a little about the city of Corinth where Paul lived for eighteen months.

Corinth is of little importance today. Only a few ruins are left of what Paul knew as a magnificent city. Then it was one of the most important places in the Roman Empire and a strategic centre in which to build a Christian church.

Have a look at the map. The narrow neck of land connecting the northern part of modern Greece (called Macedonia in the first century AD) with the southern part (then called Achaia) is only four miles across. Corinth's position on that isthmus meant all trade between the north and south passed through the city. In addition much of the sea trade from east to west (and vice versa) also passed through Corinth. In the early centuries when ships were propelled by slave oarsmen or went under sail, sailors had to make their wills before making the hazardous journey via Cape Malea on the southern tip of Achaia, and such were the dangers that the route was avoided whenever possible. Instead ships sailed up the Saronic Gulf and, if small enough, were dragged overland and refloated on the eastern side. Larger ships were unloaded and their cargoes were hauled overland and reloaded on to ships on the other side. All this trade passed through Corinth which fast became a rich, cosmopolitan city.

The city had a terrible reputation. On one of its hills stood the temple to Aphrodite which had 1,000 priestesses, 'sacred' prostitutes who plied their trade in the city.

'To live like a Corinthian' became a common saying and meant 'to live in drunken and immoral debauchery'. In this place of wealth, luxury and unmentionable vice Paul preached, and I Corinthians 6:9-11 shows us that the Gospel became the power of God to salvation for many there.

What a city! Yet London, New York or any other large present day seaport could similarly be described.

Dr. Luke in Acts 18:1-18 describes Paul's stay in Corinth. Let's read that portion and meet some of the people mentioned:

Aquilla and Priscilla (See Acts 18:18, 26; Rom. 16:3-4; I Cor. 16:19)
Paul's friendship with these two began at Corinth. Jews lived in great numbers in every city of the empire and especially in the capital, Rome. Rivalry and jealousy over their success in

trade caused Jew-hating and Jew-baiting just as it has done right through to the twenty-first century. Roman Emperors periodically issued decrees to kick all Jews out of Rome but these measures were only partially and temporarily effective. Claudius issued one such decree about 49-50 AD and Aquilla and Priscilla were among the Jews who left at that time. They were tentmakers, and Paul, who had learned that trade in his youth, met up with them and worked with them so that he could support himself while preaching the Gospel (Acts 18:4). (Strangely enough, the fact that he preached the Gospel 'free of charge' became a source of criticism among some of the Corinthian converts as we shall see when we study chapter 9.)

We can't be sure if Aquilla and Priscilla were Christians when Paul met them. Acts 2:10 tells us that Jews from Rome were present on the day of Pentecost so they may have been among the three thousand who believed on that day.

Timothy, Paul's 'beloved son' (convert) and fellow worker, came to Corinth with Silas to bring gifts from the Christians at Thessalonica and Philippi. This support enabled Paul to give himself wholly to preaching (Acts 18:5). The Philippians were generous in their support of the apostle (Phil. 4:16).

Crispus (I Cor. 1:14) was one of the few people baptised by Paul himself. (Apparently this task was usually allotted to his fellow workers.) As a leader in the synagogue Crispus had great influence which resulted in many Jews following him and becoming Christians.

Gallio (Acts 18:12-17) was Governor of the Province of Achaia. He was reputed to be virtuous and witty, and was admired as a man of exceptional fairness and calmness. His reaction to this attempt of unbelieving Jews to get rid of Paul was a very reasonable one. He was completely impartial and fair. Poor Sosthenes (v. 17) caught the backlash. The Greeks probably took advantage of the snub Gallio had administered to the Jews to express their own anti-Jewish feelings.

Apollos (Acts 18:24-28) visited Corinth. As a result of this visit (although not his fault) some of the Christians were so keen on his eloquent preaching that they formed one of the parties which spoiled the unity of the church (I Cor. 1:12).

Paul. Paul's approach to evangelism was true to the pattern of his day. Read Acts 18:4. Discussions in the synagogue took place as part of the 'Sabbath' service after readings from 'the law and the prophets'. It was usual to invite visitors to speak to the assembly (Acts 13:15) and Jesus was asked to speak in this way in his home town of Nazareth (Luke 4:16-20). Many people believed as a result of Paul's message, but opposition was sufficient to force him out of the synagogue to live and preach next door! (Acts 18:7). There he lived in the home of a Gentile which would have infuriated the unbelieving Jews even more.

The Crisis in the Corinthian Church

The letter telling Paul of the controversial problems in the Corinthian church (I Cor. 7:1; 8:1 and 12:1) reached him at Ephesus. The bearers of the letter also brought him the shattering news of the split (1:11), of an easy going attitude to immorality (5:1), disorderly worship (14:40) and of greed and drunkenness at the Lord's Supper (11:21).

The crisis (I Cor. 1:1-11) which Paul had to handle, coupled with the statement in I Corinthians 2:3 shows us that Paul, in himself, was weak and afraid of handling these tense situations and could only do so in the Lord's strength (2:4).

Sadly our Christian fellowships today are not immune from such controversies. There is no room for complacency. We should prayerfully consider those areas where we fall short before beginning to study the way Paul dealt with those matters. Doubtful issues where the Church is in error today must be faced in the light of God's Word.

We hope these glimpses of the place, people and problems of Paul's day have come alive to you and that you will see Paul's letter to the Corinthians as thoroughly applicable to the twenty-first century church.

In this study, BSB refers to the *Bible Study Book on I Corinthians – Galatians* by R. P. Martin, published by Scripture Union. Tyndale refers to *I Corinthians An Introduction and Commentary* by Leon Morris, published by The Tyndale Press.

STUDY 1

CHRISTIANS UNITED BUT THE CHURCH DIVIDED

QUESTIONS

DAY 1   *I Corinthians 1:1-3.*
a) Who appointed Paul as an apostle (Gal. 1:1)?

b) To whom did Paul write this letter?

c) Find three facts describing ALL Christians in verse 2.

DAY 2   *I Corinthians 1:1-3.*
a) What were the two things Paul wanted the Christians at Corinth to have?

b) Verse 4 is really a prayer. To whom did Paul address it?

c) How would you define 'Grace'?

DAY 3   *I Corinthians 1:4-9.*
a) For what gift of God was Paul thankful? What would this make them (2 Cor. 8:9)?

b) What had happened to the message Paul had preached to them?

DAY 4   *I Corinthians 1:4-9.*
a) What important fact about God is stated in verse 8?

QUESTIONS (contd.)

b) What does Paul say God would do for them (and you!)?

c) Why would God do this?

DAY 5 *I Corinthians 1:10-13.*
a) What had gone wrong with the church at Corinth?

b) How had Paul heard about it?

c) By what four names did the parties call themselves?

DAY 6 *I Corinthians 1:14-17.*
a) What did Christ send Paul to do?

b) How did Christ wish Paul to tell the Good News (try and put this in your own words)?

DAY 7 *I Corinthians 1:18-25.*
a) What two views are expressed about the message, or preaching of the cross (v. 18)?

b) What is it that human wisdom (cleverness) can't do?

c) What did Paul preach? Think over reasons why this is so important.

NOTES

The BODY of CHRIST is one of the New Testament names for the Church. This Body, indwelt by the Holy Spirit, is made up of all Christians, past, present and future. Paul used it of the local church at Corinth where there were divisions and other problems spoiling the life of the Body. These matters had to be dealt with.

We will learn Paul's remedies and see that we can apply them in the building up of His Body in our own local church.

The Church of God should be healthy, whole and growing. We need to be aware of factors which can bring division among us (e.g. how we worship, financial issues and a host of others), and be sensitive to the unifying work of the Holy Spirit. C. S. Lewis puts it like this: 'We must go to church for the church is not a human society of people united by their natural affinities. This is the Body of Christ in which all members, however different (and He rejoices in their differences and by no means wishes to iron them out), must share the common life, complementing and helping one another precisely by their differences.'

The word 'apostle' means 'sent one' (1:1). J. B. Phillips translates it as 'messenger'. That's good. Acts 1:21-22 suggests the qualifications for an apostle and why they were special. They were the original witnesses to all the Lord Jesus had said and done, chosen by Him to found His Church. Now ALL Christians are messengers for their Master in their own time and place.

Sosthenes may be the man named in Acts 18:17. If so, he must have become a Christian. Perhaps God used that nasty experience to open his eyes to the truth!

But isn't it fine how Paul, the apostle, associates this brother with him in sending this important letter to the Christians at Corinth? Do Christians of different calibre work together in your church? You will find other examples of this in 2 Corinthians 1:1; Philippians 1:1; Colossians 1:1; 1 Thessalonians 1:1; 2 Thessalonians 1:1.

Called out. The word 'church' (1:2) NEVER means a building in the New Testament because they were non-existent in the first century AD. Christians met in houses (1 Cor. 16:19). The Greek word translated 'church' was an ordinary, common word meaning an assembly of people of any kind. It would apply to the gathering of the citizens of a particular place to discuss its affairs. The citizens were 'called out' (that's the meaning of the Greek word) by someone like a town crier to attend at a certain time and place. Those who HEARD the call RESPONDED, went to the allotted place and thus formed the 'assembly'. Do you see how this fits our hearing God's call, responding and committing ourselves so that we become members of God's assembly, His Church?

Grace (1:3). An old definition of grace is 'God's love in action towards the undeserving'. God planned our redemption in Christ, not because we deserved it, but because He loves us with an eternal love and hates the sin that separates us from Him. Grace supplies our life with everything that delights the heart of God (see John 1:17).

Peace (1:3). Do you know there are two kinds of peace?
a) There is 'peace with God' which you can read about in Romans 5:1. This describes the peace we have when we stop rebelling against God and fighting for our own way and when we accept His forgiveness through Christ's sacrifice for us. 'Reconciled' is another word for it. This peace is a FACT irrespective of how we FEEL, or what is happening to us or around us. It is important to know that if we have turned from our own way to God and have accepted His forgiveness through Christ we HAVE this peace and NOTHING can take it from us.

b) But there is also the 'peace' which Paul writes about in Philippians 4:7. When he wrote this Paul was a prisoner at Rome, due to appear before the Emperor on trial for his life; but he knew this second kind of peace as well. This is a peace God gives His people no matter what is happening to them or around them, or what they think may happen in the future. The Holy Spirit will give it if you ask Him.

'To be revealed' and 'the day of our Lord Jesus Christ' (vv. 7-8) refer to the Second Coming of Christ. This is described in different ways but it is a wonderful fact in which every Christian can rejoice and to which every Christian can look forward.

Read more about it in John 14:3 (Jesus' promise); Acts 1:11 (God's messengers confirm it); 1 Thessalonians 4:13-17 (Paul describes what will happen).

STUDY 2

NOBODIES – PLUS GOD!

QUESTIONS

DAY 1   *I Corinthians 1:26-31.*
a) How are the church members at Corinth described?

b) How is their salvation described in these verses?

c) Why are Christians to boast in the Lord (Eph. 2:8-9)?

DAY 2   *I Corinthians 2:1-5.*
a) What was the theme of Paul's message? What did this produce (v. 5)?

b) The secret of Paul's success is in verse 4. What was it? (See the parallel for you in 2 Cor. 12:9-10.)

DAY 3   *I Corinthians 2:6-16.*
a) How many times is the Spirit mentioned in this passage?

b) How does understanding of spiritual truth come?

c) Are you relying on the Spirit to teach you? (See Jesus' promise in John 14:26; 16:13.)

QUESTIONS (contd.)

DAY 4 *I Corinthians 2:14-15; 3:1-4.*
a) What three kinds of people are mentioned in these verses? To which category did the Corinthians belong?

b) What is the 'milk' Paul speaks about here (Heb. 5:12; I Pet. 2:2)?

DAY 5 *I Corinthians 3:5-9.*
a) What produces spiritual growth?

b) Put verse 9 into your own words.

DAY 6 *I Corinthians 3:10-15.*
a) What foundation did Paul lay as he 'built' the church at Corinth?

b) How is our work for Christ to be tested, and what can be the results?

DAY 7 *I Corinthians 3:16-23.*
a) How did Paul describe the believers at Corinth?

b) How can Christians destroy this temple (look back to v. 3)?

c) Why is it futile to put confidence in men?

NOTES

If you think you are not important, not very clever, even looked down on by others, then it will encourage you to read that many of the first Christians at Corinth were 'nobodies'. Probably many of them were slaves. Although sometimes clever and educated slaves could hold quite responsible positions in a household they were still slaves, and their master could do almost anything he liked to them and with them.

Paul seeks to differentiate between 'baby' Christians (3:1-3) and Christians who quarrel as 'worldly' people do. We need to recognise Christians who are 'beginners' (described here as babes in the faith) and people who have been Christians for some time but who haven't grown spiritually. They are immature, unspiritual people who are living like those who are not Christians at all. Look up Galatians 5:16-25. Every Christian is aware of the pulls of the old sinful nature against the Holy Spirit within. Unspiritual Christians are those in whom the old nature rather than the new one predominates. If we sincerely want to 'live by the Spirit' and seek the Spirit's enabling, we will show forth the life of Christ more and more, and triumph over temptation.

In Christian service the keynote should be co-operative endeavour. Factions and fightings occur when individuals do not give the Spirit prior control of their thinking and actions. A good question for discussion: what effects do cliques in churches have on individuals, the church, the outsider? Also, relative to I Corinthians 3:12-14, it would be good to share some of the things that result in unity and progress in the life of your church.

FOUNDATIONS. Paul founded Christ's church at Corinth. He was the first to preach the Gospel there, and during his stay of eighteen months many became Christians. Apollos followed Paul in ministry there. It is not clear whether Peter ever visited the city but his name would have been well-known and a 'Peter party' could well have arisen claiming to be 'The Originals', Christians who traced their origins back to Peter rather than to Paul, the latecomer. It must have been a joy to see a Christian church planted in pagan territory. After all these centuries missionaries are still planting churches in unreached lands, but there are still many areas where the Gospel has not been preached.

Sometimes we talk about foundation members of a church, meaning those who started it. But just in case a vital truth is missed, Paul switches to the fact that the real foundation of THE Church (capital C) which is made up of all the churches or congregations of believers, is Jesus Himself. Isaiah 28:16 declares that this was God's plan, not man's. How can Christians be both 'builders' and the building? Peter gives a clue (I Pet. 2:4-10). He says Christians are living stones in God's Temple. When we, as 'living stones' co-operate with the Holy Spirit in bringing others to faith in Christ, we, too, become 'builders' of Christ's Church.

The original Greek word for temple used here means the innermost shrine where the god or goddess was supposed to live. Paul uses this word to emphasise that we are 'God's temple' because His Spirit dwells in the heart of every believer (3:16). Notice that the verb 'destroy' in 3:17, as in many places in the New Testament, does not mean to annihilate or render completely useless, but to spoil, damage badly, make less useful. Notice that God Himself will deal with anyone who will defile or destroy His temples. The devil can do nothing to undo the saving work which Christ accomplishes in a life. Nevertheless, 1 Peter 5:8-9 warns us he will seek to destroy us, but tells us how to overcome his tactics.

Be careful – watch out for attacks from Satan, your great enemy. He prowls around like a hungry, roaring lion, looking for some victim to tear apart. Stand firm when he attacks ... Trust the Lord.

Remember that other Christians all around the world are going through these tests too.

Our confidence is in the Lord and in His victory ... The Son of God appeared for this purpose: 'to destroy the devil's work' (I John 3:8).

Perhaps you should briefly discuss ways in which the evil one would try to mar your Christian testimony, and pray for one another that he will gain no foothold in your lives.

STUDY 3

HOW BIG IS YOUR FAMILY?

QUESTIONS

DAY 1 *I Corinthians 4:1-5.*
a) What have Christ's servants been put in charge of?

b) What is required of them? Who judges them?

DAY 2 *I Corinthians 4:6-7.*
a) What does Paul call the believers?

b) Who gives us everything we have?

c) Why is there no room for a Christian to boast?

DAY 3 *I Corinthians 4:8-13.*
a) According to Paul, how did the Corinthian Christians view themselves?

b) Where did it seem God had placed the apostles?

c) What 11 things did Paul suffer from?

DAY 4 *I Corinthians 4:14-21.*
a) How does Paul address the Christians here? On what authority?

QUESTIONS (contd.)

b) What has Timothy to do when he visits them?

c) What are Paul's alternatives when he comes to them?

DAY 5   *I Corinthians 5:1-5.*
a) What should the Christians have felt about the immoral member?

b) How should they have handled him? Why?

DAY 6   *I Corinthians 5:6-8.*
a) How does Paul illustrate the spread of sin?

b) What is Christ called in these verses (see also John 1:29)?

c) What does yeast or leaven represent in this passage?

DAY 7   *I Corinthians 5:9-13.*
a) What had Paul already told the Corinthians? What is he now insisting on?

b) Who will judge outsiders?

c) How are we to handle immorality in the church?

NOTES

Paul uses two different words for 'servant'. The first one means literally the slave who rowed on the lower bank of a large ship, a most dangerous place. It came to mean anyone who did any kind of unskilled, menial job. The other word is 'steward' and means the owner's deputy, a very important, skilled job. Christians are BOTH in their work for the Lord.

Paul quite often exhorts (4:6) other Christians to follow his example (see I Cor. II:1 and I Thess. I:6). Would you dare to say this to a young convert?

In 4:18 there is another reference to what seems to have been a distinguishing mark of the Christians at Corinth – 'arrogance' or 'swollen with pride' as one translation puts it. Had it to do with the fact that they belonged to such an important city (see 4:6, 19; 5:2; 13:4)?

'Immorality' - Sexual laxity was rife amongst the first century Greeks but ... the Christian attitude to the prevailing practice and thought was one of uncompromising opposition (Tyndale). Paul was shocked that something (it is not quite clear what, though it seems to have been some form of incestuous relationship) was being permitted in the church which was not countenanced even by pagan society in general (5:1-3). Christians today need to be aware that Western society is no better than first century Greek society. Time Magazine reported some time ago that there was a pressure group in the USA campaigning for the legalisation of incestuous relationships, particularly between parents and children on the grounds that it could be beneficial! There is only one safe attitude for the Christian and it is summed up in this quotation: 'We must never fall into lukewarmness (as the Christians at Corinth had done) towards evil or evil men. There is no power or safety for us except in the heart, cold towards the enticement of wrong and hot in resentment against it.' We need to pray the words taught to boys in a famous school, 'Oh God, whom none can love except they hate the thing that is evil ... deliver us when we are tempted to look on sin without abhorrence.'

Handing over to Satan (5:5) probably means to excommunicate from the church since 'outside the church is the sphere of Satan' (Tyndale). How the destruction of the individual's body ('flesh') should follow is not clear except that in some instances there are physical consequences of spiritual failings (11:30).

Paul makes reference here to the Lord's Second Coming (5:5). When He does come He will judge His servants. He will take into account our secret thoughts, desires, deeds and motives.

'The yeast of malice and wickedness' (5:8). Look up Matthew 13:33. There Jesus' parable on 'yeast' or 'leaven' is a picture of the good influence of the spreading of the Kingdom of God as opposed to I Corinthians 5:7 where it typifies SIN.

'Ten thousand guardians' (4:15). This sounds like a colloquial exaggeration just as we say 'crowds of ...' or even 'millions of ...' when we simply mean an unusually large number. This is one of the reminders that Paul was writing a real letter. The guardians or teachers were slaves who, under the direction of the fathers, superintended the welfare of the children. The Christian, under his Master, Christ, should be seeking the spiritual welfare of his spiritual children or of any young Christians for whom he is responsible. We need to remember that Wesley said that to have spiritual children and not provide for their teaching and training was like 'begetting children for the murderer'. (Jesus called the devil a murderer – John 8:44.)

SUFFERING FOR CHRIST'S SAKE. The picture in I Corinthians 4:9 is that of condemned criminals being punished by fighting wild animals to the death; so men of God are 'made a spectacle' in the battle for the souls of others.

Read and think about Paul's own sufferings listed in 2 Corinthians 6:4-10 and 11:23-29. Although we may only have to face average trials and difficulties, Christians in some lands today suffer like this and from even worse tortures invented by our so-called progressive civilisation. Evil evolves along with 'progress' in technology. Here is a prayer from the story of Florence Allshom which we can all pray: 'I want people to see Thee, O Lord, when they find me in a perfectly hopeless situation. If I can show Thee working in the background of all that happened, that will be enough.'

THE IMPORTANCE OF DISCIPLING OTHERS. The Christians at Corinth were not only Paul's harvest field and building (3:9) but his spiritual children (4:14). Paul has been severely ironical (4:6-13), but now he sounds a wooing note and directs a tender appeal to them as 'my dear children' (BSB). Parents understand there is need for different tones and approaches in coping with naughty children.

STUDY 4

TO WHOM DO YOU BELONG?

QUESTIONS

DAY 1   *I Corinthians 6:1-11.*
a) What mistake were the Corinthians making? What advice did Paul give them?

b) Discuss how their lives had been changed by the Spirit of God (v. 11).

DAY 2   *I Corinthians 6:12-17.*
a) 'I am allowed to do anything' (v. 12). How did Paul respond to this apparent attitude of the Corinthians?

b) What important fact is to regulate a Christian's behaviour?

c) What great promise is stated in verse 14 (more of this in ch. 15)?

DAY 3   *I Corinthians 6:18-20.*
a) How does Paul describe the Christian's body?

b) What price was paid to enable us to belong to God (I Pet. 1:18-19)?

DAY 4   *I Corinthians 7:1-7.*
a) What does Paul teach here about marriage (v. 2)? And about sexual relations (vv. 3-4)?

QUESTIONS (contd.)

b) For what reasons may a couple deny themselves their normal sexual relationship?

c) How does Paul look on his single state?

DAY 5   *I Corinthians 7:8-11.*
a) What advice does Paul give to the unmarried and widows?

b) Is divorce allowed because of differences between Christian husbands and wives?

DAY 6   *I Corinthians 7:12-16.*
a) Define the instructions for a Christian husband/wife married to an unbelieving spouse. What could happen to the non-Christian partner?

b) What is said about children when one parent becomes a Christian?

DAY 7   *I Corinthians 7:17-24.*
a) How should a Christian person live after conversion? Do you see an exception to this rule in verse 21?

b) All Christians are slaves. Whose?

Spiritual issues cannot be settled legally (I Cor. 6:1-11)

The great temple had many functions in addition to being a place of worship. It was a bank and also a court of law.

Paul's criticism wasn't that the Corinthians wouldn't get justice in civil courts, but that they were looking in the wrong place for solutions (6:1). Jesus had given instruction on how Christians were to handle disagreements among themselves (see Matt. 18:15-17). How far is this practised in your church fellowship?

A single man comments on marriage (I Cor. 7:1-16)

There is good cause for putting 'It is good for a man not to marry' (7:1) in inverted commas as a quotation from a letter to Paul (7:1), otherwise it would look as if Paul was contradicting what he wrote elsewhere. The BSB comments 'The apostle who wrote Ephesians 5:21-23 is not likely to have expressed a stark condemnation of conjugal union.' The Tyndale commentary is most helpful on this passage commenting on verse 7: 'marriage, just as much as celibacy, is a gift from God', and on verse 9: 'Paul does not regard the suppression of sexual desire as itself meritorious, as some later writers have held'.

Paul's suggestion (7:5) that marriage partners abstain from sexual relations in order to spend more time in prayer is echoed in this quotation 'Fasting represents an attitude of detachment from the things of time and sense whether it be food or pleasure or lawful ambition. Prayer represents the complementary attitude of attachment to the things of God. We shall readily determine, under the guidance of the Holy Spirit, what particular forms our fastings shall take to help spiritual development' (Griffith Thomas).

The issue of one spouse in a non-Christian marriage becoming a Christian is clearly dealt with here. The Christian partner has a responsibility to remain true to the marriage vows (v. 20). The indication is that a life lived out to God's glory could be the means of the other partner becoming a Christian. Regarding children being 'holy' because of a parent being a Christian, the BSB suggests that it means 'brought within the sphere of God's grace', that is, a godly parent will pray for such children and lay a foundation of God's Word in their lives. This is a fearful and wonderful responsibility.

Who owns your body (I Cor. 6:15-20 and 7:20-23)**?**

Paul's teaching about the body is authoritative. If a Christian is to live for God's glory then he has to face up to issues – issues of eating versus gluttony, sleep, etc.

What is it, this seamless body stocking, some ten yards square, our casing, our facade, that flushes, pales, perspires, glistens, glows, furrows, tingles, cracks, itches, pleasures and pains us all our days; at once keeper of the organs within, a sensitive probe and adventurer into the world outside?' (Richard Selzer).

For the Christian, it is the Temple of God, the Holy Spirit. We, our bodies, souls and spirits, belong to God twice over. We are His by right of creation (Gen. 1:27; Jer. 1:5) and by right of purchase (1 Cor. 6:20 and 7:23).

Point to ponder:
'God used to have a temple for His people. Now He has people as His temple' (1 Cor. 6:19).

STUDY 5

IF IT'S DOUBTFUL – DON'T

QUESTIONS

DAY 1 *I Corinthians 7:24-40 (Phillips' translation is helpful).*
a) What general advice did Paul give for living in that difficult era and environment?

b) What is the aim of a Christian spouse regarding his or her partner? What is the basic criterion for Christian marriage?

DAY 2 *I Corinthians 8:1-6.*
a) Discuss what Paul says here about knowledge and love.

b) How does Paul contrast idols and God?

c) How is Jesus described?

DAY 3 *I Corinthians 8:7-13.*
a) Why would some Christians be harmed by eating, or seeing others eat food that had been offered to idols?

b) Can you write a resolution such as Paul made in verse 13?

DAY 4 *I Corinthians 9:1-7.*
a) What did Paul indicate as being essential to being an apostle (v. 1; Acts 1:21-22)?

b) Paul claimed two 'rights' which the other apostles had. What were they (vv. 3-6)?

c) What three jobs did Paul use as an illustration of his service?

DAY 5 *I Corinthians 9:8-12.*
a) On what law of God did Paul base his right to support as a Christian worker (Deut. 25:4)?

b) What did he say about farm labourers?

c) Why should Paul likewise be supported?

DAY 6 *I Corinthians 9:12-18.*
a) Compare verse 13 with Luke 10:7. Try to state this teaching in your own words.

b) What was Paul's great privilege? He repeated it three times.

c) What was his salary (v. 18)?

DAY 7 *I Corinthians 9:19-23.*
a) What was Paul's chief aim? Is it yours?

b) How did Paul live among the Jews and the Gentiles?

c) Whose law was Paul under?

Should I or should I not (I Cor. 8)?

It is strange that this question of whether Christians should eat meat which had been offered to idols should arise at all. Paul had been involved in a similar issue (see Acts 15 especially vv. 2 and 29) when the decision had been taken for the church at Antioch (and thus was relevant to all Gentiles who became Christians) to abstain.

Three different situations arose out of the common practice of offering meat offerings as sacrifices to gods in the heathen temples.

1. Sometimes the worshippers with family and friends would share in a meal at the temple which consisted of part of the animal sacrifice. Members of the same trade or profession also held such feasts. There is a comparable custom in many western countries today to hold banquets or dinners, but the meal has no religious meaning. In Paul's day there was often the free distribution of surplus meat to the poor, and since many of the Corinthian Christians were poor they could have been in this 'handout'.
2. Christians could be invited for a meal to the home of a friend where the meat might have come from the temple offerings.
3. Meat, surplus to the temple requirements, was sold in shops, so Christians could unknowingly buy it.

Should those Christians sever family and friendly relationships because of all this?

How were they to maintain links that would win them for Christ? Jesus Himself accepted invitations into homes of doubtful characters, e.g. Matthew (Matt. 9:9-13) and Zacchaeus (Luke 19:2-7) thus giving rise to criticism (Luke 15:1-2).

Throughout the ages there have been Christians who have gone to extremes in 'separating themselves' in an attempt to be beyond reproach, but without human contact with the world we cannot reach souls for Christ.

The problem of 'food sacrificed to idols' (8:4) may not arise in our culture, but it is still a problem in other countries today. However, we need to examine our lives frequently to ensure we are not indulging in things which could be a hindrance to others.

A. W. Tozer wrote: '... an evil disposition manifested by a Christian does the church more harm than anything a non-Christian can do. Here are a few of them; touchiness, irritability, churlishness, faultfinding, peevishness, temper, resentfulness, cruelty, uncharitable attitudes....'

Someone else has written 'See that your RIGHT does not lead others astray and that it does not do violence to that most sacred and delicate thing, a human conscience.'

When we hurt others, we hurt Christ

Christ is affected by the hurts and offences we inflict against those for whom He died. (8:12) Read Acts 9:3-5. Paul was persecuting the Christians but the Lord said that he was persecuting Him. Paul came out of this encounter a new man with a sensitive spirit. May the Lord likewise make all of us sensitive to the needs of others through sensitivity to Him.

God given authority (I Cor. 9:1-23)

Some questioned Paul's apostleship since he wasn't one of the original twelve. Christians are so prone to denigrate fellow Christians and become the devil's tools to destroy fellowship and cause division in the church.

The Corinthians suggested that Paul did not exercise his right to financial support from the church because he was unsure of his apostleship. But Paul testified clearly that he had seen the Lord (i.e. knew Divine commissioning for his task) and claimed the Christians at Corinth as the fruit of his apostleship. Chapter 15 will tell us more of Paul's convictions on this matter.

Paul's illustration of the unmuzzled ox (a God-given rule – see Deut. 18:1) is very graphic. Paul was a worker for souls. We see his deep concern for the lost in the verb 'win' used five times in verses 19-22. He was both a fisherman (finding the lost) and a shepherd (caring for their souls). Paul was 'all things to all men' (v. 22). This doesn't mean he compromised himself before the world. He identified with them where they were so that he might bring them to what they should be in Christ. Look again at the title of this week's study. It is based on Romans 14:23. Compare it with Paul's conclusion in I Corinthians 9:23.

Certainty of 'rightness' that is, acting in faith, will keep you from backsliding and ensure you don't cause others to stumble.

To help you understand: Conscience is our 'awareness' of what is morally good or bad (Acts 23:1; I Tim. 1:5; Heb. 13:18). A weak conscience is one not enlightened enough (through God's truth) to be able to distinguish between what is lawful or unlawful (I Cor. 8:7, 10, 12). A good conscience is therefore an enlightened conscience, sensitive to the Lord and discerning between right and wrong (Acts 23:1; Rom. 2:15).

STUDY 6

WINNERS – OR ALSO-RANS?

QUESTIONS

DAY 1   *I Corinthians 9:24-27.*
a) What does a runner do to become a winner?

b) Why did Paul keep his body under control (2 Tim. 2:5; 4:7-8)?

DAY 2   *I Corinthians 10:1-5.*
a) Make a list of the blessings the Israelites received.

b) What was God's verdict on them?

DAY 3   *I Corinthians 10:6-13.*
a) List the things Paul said we are not to do.

b) Why was Israel's history recorded?

c) What do we learn here about tests and temptations?

DAY 4   *I Corinthians 10:14-17.*
a) What prohibition is repeated in this passage? (Ask God to show you anything, even legitimate things, which you hold more dearly than your Lord.)

QUESTIONS (contd.)

b) What happens when believers take part in the Lord's Supper?

DAY 5   *I Corinthians 10:18-22.*
a) What was part of the worship of the Israelites (v. 18; Lev. 19:6)?

b) To whom are the sacrifices in heathen temples offered?

c) What could happen to a Christian sharing in heathen feasts (v. 20)?

DAY 6   *I Corinthians 10:23–11:1.*
a) Whose interests should a Christian put first?

b) What was the rule for Christians at Corinth when buying meat?

c) What was the rule when invited to a meal in a non-Christian home?

d) When must Christians NOT eat the meat?

DAY 7   *I Corinthians 11:2-16.*
a) For what did Paul praise the Corinthian Christians?

b) What did Paul say was the custom in all the churches for both men and women?

c) What was Paul's instruction to an argumentative Christian (v. 16)?

NOTES

Restful assurance and godly fear (I Cor. 10:1-5)

It looks as if the Corinthian Christians expected salvation to be automatically guaranteed because they observed the sacraments of baptism and the Lord's Supper. Paul pointed out that the Israelites enjoyed their sacraments (v. 2) yet as they turned aside to idolatry and became apostate, they quickly met their fate (vv. 5-10). The New Testament emphasises two things that are important in our Christian life:

Confidence in God	A Godly Reverence
Romans 8:28-39;	Hebrews 6:4-9; 10:19-39; 12:25
Philippians 1:6	2 Peter 1:10; I Corinthians 9:27

There is no room for complacency. If assurance breeds a careless attitude our moral senses will be dulled, so it is good to recall these warnings.

Provision from God (I Cor. 10:4)

God met the needs of the Israelites supplying both food (manna Exod. 16:14-15) and water (Exod. 17:6). When Paul spoke of the 'rock' that went with them (v. 4) he didn't mean a literal, movable rock. He was recognising Christ with them and supplying their needs. In type, this provision for Israel indicates the spiritual blessings we have in Christ. He guides, feeds, helps and delivers us from evil as we put our trust in Him.

Strengthened through testing (I Cor. 10:12-13)

After stressing Israel's failures Paul anticipated two possible and opposite reactions.

1. Some would say: 'That would never happen to me!' and we find Paul's answer to that in verse 12.
2. Others would say: 'If that happened to God's chosen people, what chance have I got?' Paul's answer is in verse 13. God really does know our limits. He won't allow us to be overwhelmed. If you are teaching a child to swim you will gradually let him go unsupported, but you will never let him drown.

Remember, the tempter has to get permission before assailing us (Luke 22:31-32) and as others have conquered temptation, so can we (Heb. 4:15).

Giving the devil a foothold (I Cor. 10:11-21)

Paul goes back again to the issue of eating meat offered to idols. Look back to the notes on Study 5. Here the emphasis is on a Christian entering into liaison with idolators at a temple feast. A Christian must not do this. 'The awful consequence is that such a liaison may open the door to demonic influence' (BSB). Those who participate in the Christian feast of remembrance should have no part in heathen feasts (vv. 16, 21). A true story from the Mau Mau war in Kenya vividly illustrates verse 21. A Christian woman with a noose around her neck was threatened with hanging unless she drank the blood of the Mau Mau oath. She refused, crying 'I have drunk the blood of Jesus, how can I drink the Mau Mau cup?' She was hanged.

Today there is much dabbling in magic and witchcraft. Don't do it.

Leith Samuel wrote: 'Magic is out! Everything which is used in connection with magic or the occult we should steer clear of: astrology, horoscopes, amulets, charms, automatic writing, ouija boards, planchettes, glass moving, cartomacy, palmistry, divining rods, mirror magic, crystal ball gazing, clairvoyance and other forms of mechanistic fortune telling.'

Getting down to practicalities

Paul was pretty forthright as he started to deal with problem issues in the church at Corinth. The issue of head coverings was obviously causing contention. In the West, at the beginning of the twentieth century, no respectable woman would have attended public worship without wearing a hat. Ladies always wore a hat in public. Today customs have changed and very few women wear hats in the street or in church. With men it is different. Whatever way they dress, it would be regarded as insulting if a man wore a hat in church. However, customs vary across the world. The key to harmony in these issues is in chapter 14:40 (also 10:24, 30-33; 11:1).

In Bible times it was customary for women to be covered (head and face) in public.

Only prostitutes (and there were many in Corinth) ventured on the street without a veil. Since the church met in homes, the question was whether this was a 'public' occasion or not. If so, women should be veiled. If not, they need not be covered.

Jewish men have always been accustomed to covering their head at prayer, but Christian men in the first century adopted the practice of not covering their heads.

The important issue is to preserve unity and order in a public assembly. Paul is careful to point out that the issue of headship is not one of authority and domination, but the imparting of resources of love, wisdom and strength without which the highest for men and women cannot be realised (1 Cor. 11:8-12).

STUDY 7

IS IT THE LORD'S TABLE?

QUESTIONS

DAY 1   *I Corinthians 11:17-22.*
a) What was Paul's verdict on the Christian meetings for worship at Corinth?

b) Name the two faults mentioned (vv. 18, 21). What did the second one lead to?

c) What two things were the Christians in danger of doing (v. 22)?

DAY 2   *I Corinthians 11:23-26.*
a) Where did Paul get his teaching on the Lord's Supper from?

b) What two things are symbolised in this Supper?

c) How long are Christians to go on having the Supper?

DAY 3   *I Corinthians 11:26-34.*
a) What should Christians do BEFORE sharing in the Supper? Why?

b) What forms may God's judgment take?

c) How can the situation in verse 21 be avoided?

DAY 4   *I Corinthians 12:1-3.*
a) What subject does Paul start to deal with here?

QUESTIONS (contd.)

b) What had been their 'religious' experience before conversion (v. 2)?

c) How would someone claiming to speak by the Holy Spirit be recognised as genuine?

DAY 5   *I Corinthians 12:4-11.*
a) What should be the result of the Spirit's presence in a Christian's life (v. 7)?

b) Make a list of the ways the Spirit works through individual Christians (vv. 7-10).

c) Who decides what gift any individual Christian will have?

DAY 6   *I Corinthians 12:12-20.*
a) What racial and social differences were there among the Christians at Corinth (v. 13)?

b) Who makes Christians part of Christ's body?

c) Why is the human body like it is?

DAY 7   *I Corinthians 12:12-31.*
a) Try to give a simple summary of Paul's teaching concerning the human and Christ's body in these verses.

b) What happens if one part of the body suffers?

c) What do all Christians make up?

More harm than good!

It is sad to think of the divisive party spirit and gluttony which appeared to mark the so-called 'Lord's Supper' in the church at Corinth (I Cor. II:17-22). The 'church' would have met in a house and the meal would have been a fellowship time during which a communion service was held. It should have been a time when the oneness of the church (symbolised by a single loaf) was displayed and realised to the full. Instead, rich members arrived early, ate a hearty meal, drank too much wine, and left little or nothing for the workers (slaves) who remained embarrassed and hungry. Probably these people were too poor to contribute to the meal.

This behaviour disgusted Paul, as it would us today. Yet are we beyond reproach? Do we contribute to divisive issues within our church fellowships? The communion service used today prohibits excess in the house of God, but how disciplined are our eating habits anyway? Are we more concerned about our physical needs than our spiritual food? What we are our church fellowship and witness are. Do we bring honour or dishonour to the Lord? The Corinthians were displeasing the Lord and despising the church by their behaviour.

Exalting the Lord (II:23-34)

Paul wasn't present at the Lord's Supper (which was also the Feast) but he says (vv. 23-25) that the Lord Himself had directly taught him its significance, giving him the words of institution.

(For other examples of special revelation to Paul see Acts I8:9; 22:18; 26:14-16; 27:23-25; Gal. I:12; 2:2; 2 Cor. I2:7).

Just as the Passover feast brought a reliving of the Israelites' deliverance, so at the Lord's Table the Christian relives the events of His redemption, remembering the Upper Room, the Cross, the Empty Tomb, and rejoicing in anticipation of the Lord's Return. Paul points out the importance of heart preparation for this feast, so that we come to the Table with a good conscience (v. 28) and do not incur judgment upon ourselves (v. 30). If each of us participates in this way, the unity of the body will not be destroyed and Christ will be exalted.

In a very real way we are His body. Dr. Paul Brand comments: 'Jesus departed leaving no body on earth to exhibit the Spirit of God to an unbelieving world (as He had done during His earthly ministry), except for the faltering, bumbling community of followers who had largely forsaken Him at His death. WE are what Jesus left on earth. He did not leave a book or doctrinal statement, or a system of religious thought; He left a visible community to embody Him and represent Him to the world ... The metaphor, Body of Christ, hinted at by Him and fully expounded by Paul, could only arise AFTER Jesus Christ had left this earth. Paul's words about the body were addressed to people at Corinth and elsewhere, whom he assailed for human frailty. He did not say the people are like a Body of Christ, but that in every place we are the Body of Christ. The Spirit has come and dwelt among us and the world knows an invisible God mainly by our "enfleshment" of Him.'

The founder of WEC International said 'I live for the day when I see Jesus Christ walking the Congo forest in black bodies.' Today, that dream has become a reality – the Church of God in that land is strong with thousands of believers.

SPIRITUAL GIFTS

To possess spiritual gifts is one thing; to set them in order of priority and use them worthily is another' (BSB).

Paul says four things concerning the gifts of the Spirit (I Cor. 12:1-12):

1. Since every Christian is indwelt by the Holy Spirit, each is endowed and fitted for useful service of the Lord by the power of God within the fellowship of the church. Therefore every member is important though none is indispensable.
2. There is a rich variety of gifts of which nine are specifically mentioned.
3. Lest anyone should assess that the lack of a spectacular gift (in human terms) was a sign of disfavour, the apostle says the Spirit gives as 'he determines' (v. II). This is very important as some say today that a Christian lacking a certain gift is not Spirit filled.
4. Gifts are 'for the common good' (v. 7) i.e. for the spiritual building up of the church. (See also 14:12 and Eph. 4:12-16.)

This diversity of gifts doesn't therefore destroy the unity of the church, but transforms it into a living organism which pulsates with life – the 'common life in the body of Christ' (BSB). We should guard against differences regarding the gifts of God's Spirit lest they result in division rather than unity.

It is also tragic that the beautiful original Greek word 'charisma' meaning gifts of the Spirit has been taken over by the world, misused and spoilt by application to athletes, pop stars, politicians etc. We need to cling to its Biblical meaning. Michael Harper in *Let My People Grow* writes 'The word Charisma could be defined as the sovereign gift of God the Spirit to a man or woman to be and to do what God has called them to be and do in the service to the Body of Christ and the world.'

STUDY 8

LOVE! SACRIFICIAL DEVOTION OR IDLE SENTIMENT?

QUESTIONS

DAY 1   *I Corinthians 12:31–13:3.*
a) Did Paul say, 'And now I will show you the best gift of all'?

b) Make a list of the five things which are useless without love.

c) Think this over: 'The best speech of earth or heaven without love is but noise whether you are a speaker or a listener.

DAY 2   *I Corinthians 13:4-7.*
a) Write down the two things love is (v. 4a) and the eight things love is not (vv. 4b-6) and the four things love does all the time (v. 7).

b) Remind yourself that such love was once incarnate in a human life like yours by reading these verses again substituting 'Jesus' for 'love'. Now let God speak to you. Read them over a third time putting in your own name instead of 'love'.

DAY 3   *I Corinthians 13:8-13.*
a) What is eternal or permanent?

b) List the three things which are incomplete and will pass away.

c) What three things remain? Which is the greatest?

DAY 4   *I Corinthians 14:1-6.*
a) What two gifts is Paul writing about?

QUESTIONS (contd.)

b) Whom does the person speaking in tongues help?

c) Whom does the person proclaiming God's message help?

DAY 5   *I Corinthians 14:7-17.*
a) What is important to do when speaking in church?

b) What was Paul's vision for the church (v. 12)?

c) When can others fully identify (say 'Amen') to our prayers (vv. 15-16)?

DAY 6   *I Corinthians 14:18-25.*
a) What would Paul prefer to do in the church?

b) What will an ordinary person or unbeliever think if they hear people speaking in tongues?

c) Write out the five things which may happen to an ordinary person or unbeliever when they hear God's message.

DAY 7   *I Corinthians 14:26-33.*
a) List the five 'items' mentioned in the meeting for worship. What MUST every item do?

b) What should happen if there is nobody present to interpret tongues? Who may speak God's message? And how many at a time?

NOTES

Love is the Greatest (I Cor. 13)

'The purpose of this great chapter is often not fully appreciated. This purpose is to show that whilst the Corinthians were to be commended for seeking the greatest gifts of the Spirit (12:31; 14:12), any gift is valueless unless it is accompanied by love. Love is NOT one of the gifts which a Christian may or may not have; it is the indispensable disposition or attitude without which all the gifts combined are misdirected and in vain. It is a question, therefore, of love PLUS whatever endowment of the Holy Spirit we may have received. Gifts are always to be exercised under the control and direction of love.'

Soft Sentimentality v Unselfish Love

It has been said that love is a ragbag of a word. It is used loosely in all kinds of ways. 'I love pie and chips' or 'I love my dog' or 'I love that scenery' and so on.

For many people today it stands for soft sentimentality and various expressions of the sex instinct. When Paul was writing his letters he had a similar problem. He could not use the ordinary Greek word which meant 'possessive love'. He used a word 'Agape' which means the deliberate accomplishment of an unselfish purpose. Love has to be learned. All men are loveable although they are not all likeable. This is how we can love an enemy. It doesn't mean liking him, having feelings of affection for him, but seeking his highest good. Love is a duty commanded by Jesus. As suggested above, our word 'love' has been taken over, smeared with secularist overtones and returned to us almost too soiled for Christian use. This is true of other words such as dedication, commitment, conversion and charisma. We have no other word we can use in English so that frequently we find ourselves talking about 'Christian love', the love we see in the life and death of Christ.

Paul writes that this kind of love 'always protects, always trusts, always hopes, always perseveres.' This positive translation of the NIV is better than the negative one of other versions (vv. 4-6).

Tyndale's commentary has a good note about 'hope'. 'The thought is not that of an unrealistic optimism which fails to take account of realities. It is rather a refusal to take failure as final.' That is the Christian hope of the New Testament. We need hope like that when seeking to win the lost; when all our endeavours seem to have failed (v. 7).

True Reflections

Mirrors were once made of polished metal. Corinth was famous for those they produced. Even the best quality ones, which few Christians would have been able to afford, would have given a very imperfect reflection. Try it. Look into an ordinary mirror and then into a polished tin lid. This will help you understand the GNB translation 'the dim image' (13:12).

An Eternal Triangle! But love is still pre-eminent (13:13)

Faith – Hope – Love – are mentioned together elsewhere in the New Testament and evidently formed a well-known triad. Study the other references (Rom. 5:1-5; Gal. 5:5-6; Eph. 4:2-3; Col. 1:4-5; 1 Thess. 1:3; 5:8).

The writer of BSB suggests that the second half of this verse should be translated 'but greater than these (faith, hope, love) is 'THE LOVE'. This is a literal translation of the Greek so that THE LOVE would refer to God's love shown in Christ.' It's a helpful thought!

'Put love first' expresses in a nutshell what Paul has to say at the conclusion of his discussion on love's pre-eminence and permanence. Once this is done, the believers should not be slothful or lacking in spiritual ambition but seek to be the very best for God by using to the full whatever endowment the Spirit has granted.' BSB.

Understanding results in Edification

Paul sums up his directions with two simple rules.

1. Do everything to edify, to build up individual Christian character (14:26).
2. Do everything in a decent and orderly fashion (14:40).

Worship is to be orderly so that the 'body' may be strengthened (1 Cor. 14:26, 40). Teaching, to be edifying, must be understood (14:3-6, 12, 19).

Outsiders and enquirers after the truth are not to be confused by tongues, but convicted and convinced through the Word (14:16, 23-25). There was a strong tendency in the Corinthian church to stress the use of tongues. Paul emphasised the greater importance of 'edifying the soul in truth' – giving comfort, consolation and encouragement to growth in the Lord (14:3). This glimpse (v. 26) of the pattern or content of Christian meetings in Paul's day is about the only one given us. 1 Thessalonians 5:16-22 and Ephesians 5:19 add a little more to the picture.

It would be fitting after this study to sing or recite together prayerfully this relevant verse:

Let there be love shared among us, let there be love in our eyes,
May now Your love sweep this nation, cause us, O Lord, to arise.
Give us a fresh understanding of brotherly love that is real,
Let there be love shared among us, let there be love.

STUDY 9

CHRISTIAN HOPE

QUESTIONS

DAY 1 *1 Corinthians 14:34-40.*
a) What did Paul say about the behaviour of women in the church?

b) Why should what Paul has written be taken seriously?

c) How are things to be done in the church?

DAY 2 *1 Corinthians 15:1-7.*
a) What facts are stated about the Gospel in verses 1-2?

b) How is the Gospel summarised in verses 3-4?

c) What evidence is there in these verses for the resurrection of Jesus Christ?

DAY 3 *1 Corinthians 15:8-11.*
a) How does Paul describe his conversion experience (Acts 9:3-6)?

b) Why did he say he did not deserve to be called an apostle (Acts 8:3)?

c) To think over: Can you echo Paul's words, 'by the grace of God I am what I am'?

QUESTIONS (contd.)

DAY 4   *1 Corinthians 15:12-19.*
a) What were some of these Christians saying (v. 12)? How did Paul show that this was impossible?

b) Discuss some of the consequences if Christ had not risen from the dead (vv. 14-18).

DAY 5   *1 Corinthians 15:20-28.*
a) What does Christ's resurrection guarantee?

b) Through whom does resurrection become possible?

c) When will those who belong to Christ and have fallen asleep (i.e. died) rise?

d) What is the last enemy to be destroyed?

DAY 6   *1 Corinthians 15:29-34.*
a) How did Paul summarise the extent of his sufferings in his ministry (v. 31)?

b) Why was he prepared to put up with this?

DAY 7   *1 Corinthians 15:35-44.*
a) What questions do some have about the resurrection?

b) To what does Paul compare our dying and being raised (vv. 36-38)?

c) Try to put verses 39-44 into your own words.

NOTES

Special advice to women (14:34-39)
Look back to I Corinthians 11:5 which clearly shows that a woman's participation in prayer and ministry is recognised. Why then this injunction from Paul (v. 34)? There are two possible meanings.

First, thoughtless chatter (even if they wanted to ask a relevant question) was inappropriate. Secondly, the verb 'chatter' is the same as the word used for 'speaking in tongues' and Paul may have had the latter in mind, stressing that this should not happen if there was no one present to interpret (14:27-28).

Changed by the grace of God (15:1-10)
'The Twelve' (though with the death of Judas they were only eleven) is descriptive of the disciples who companied with Jesus. In Luke 6:13 Jesus, Himself, termed these 'twelve' the apostles. Paul's apostleship was called into question because he had not been one of the 'close-in' team with Jesus. In describing his late encounter with Jesus he uses a word of abuse – bastard. Paul's enemies may also have used it of him because his personal appearance was anything but handsome (if we are to believe early tradition). No doubt Paul felt it descriptive of his violent and late birth into the apostolic family. But he acknowledges what the grace of God has accomplished in blessing him and changing the direction of his life (v. 10).

> 'I am not what I **ought** to be,
> I am not what I **wish** to be,
> I am not what I **hope** to be,
> Yet I can truly say
> I am not what I once was.'
>   (John Newton)

A fallacy condemned
Paul hardly felt the issue of baptising for the dead needed an answer! Perhaps there was scorn or pity in his voice as he asked the questions which revealed his conviction about the matter (15:29). Read the verse aloud with the appropriate tone in your voice. You might find yourself agreeing!

The right sense of value (15:32)
Paul made it clear that he was expending his life in the right direction. When he referred to the wild beasts of Ephesus he was, no doubt, referring not to beasts, but to evil men. (GNB puts 'beasts' in italics to indicate this.) Barclay says that a Roman citizen (which Paul was) could not be condemned to fight in the arena with animals, although we know this did happen

to some. Paul was in great danger at some point in Ephesus (2 Cor. 1:8-9). A Christian leader writing in the second century mentions 'fighting with wild beasts' but makes it clear he is referring to ill-treatment by soldiers.

Christians down the centuries have suffered for Christ's sake. Oz Guinness quotes the uncouth schoolboy joke about Christians being like runner beans, never better than when tied to a stake! The story of the church proves that 'the blood of the martyrs is the seed of the church'.

We know of the dying witness of Katar Singh, a Tibetan Christian. He was sewn up to the neck in a wet yak skin and left to be crushed to death as the skin contracted in the heat of a blazing sun.

He said:

I give to Him who gave to me my life, my all, His all to be;
My debt to Him, how can I pay though I may live to endless day.
I ask not one, but thousand lives for Him and His own sacrifice;
Will I then not gladly die for Jesus' sake and ask not why?

That night, it is said, a leading official in the Lama's palace became a believer.

Wrong belief (15:33-4)

The vehemence of these two verses shows how deeply Paul felt about wrong belief which in this case was the denial of the resurrection. Paul's application of the well-known saying he quoted is that keeping the wrong kind of company can corrupt our Christian habits and belief. There is a connection between WHAT and HOW we believe. In a broadcast programme one woman expressed this popular, but erroneous view: 'It doesn't matter WHAT people believe as long as they LIVE GOOD LIVES!' Error arises basically from lack of a real knowledge of God. 'Doctrine leads to CONDUCT and unsound doctrine leads to SINFUL BEHAVIOUR' (Tyndale). What we believe – we are. See what Jesus says about it in Mark 12:24. Keep hiding God's Word in your heart (Ps. 119:11).

STUDY 10
TERMINAL OR TRIUMPHAL
QUESTIONS

DAY 1 *1 Corinthians 15:42-50.*
a) How is the body described before and after the resurrection?

b) How is Jesus, the last Adam, described?

c) Whose likeness will believers have after the resurrection?

d) What is impossible for 'flesh and blood'?

DAY 2 *1 Corinthians 15:51-58.*
a) We may not all die – but what will happen when the last trumpet sounds?

b) What did Paul give thanks to God for?

c) What were the Christians at Corinth to keep busy in?

d) What is true of all service for the Lord?

DAY 3 *1 Corinthians 16:1-4.*
What lessons can we learn from Paul's instructions about Christian giving?

DAY 4 *1 Corinthians 16:5-9.*
a) Where did Paul plan to go?

QUESTIONS (contd.)

b) What condition did Paul attach to visiting Corinth?

c) Why did he wish to stay on at Ephesus for a time?

DAY 5   *1 Corinthians 16:10-12.*
a) How were they to treat Timothy and why?

b) What did Paul call Apollos?

c) What had Paul encouraged him to do?

DAY 6   *1 Corinthians 16:13-18.*
a) Find the five injunctions in verses 13 and 14. Now let God use them to search your heart.

b) How did Paul describe Stephanas and his family?

c) What had Stephanas, Fortunatus and Achaicus done?

DAY 7   *1 Corinthians 16:19-24.*
a) List the people and churches who sent greetings.

b) How were the believers to greet each other?

c) Upon whom did Paul call down a curse?

d) What did Paul pray for the Corinthian church?

What a contrast (15:42-49)

Our human inheritance in Adam leaves us with bodies which are weak, dying and subject to sin (Rom. 6:12-13). In Christ, the last Adam, we shall, by His Spirit, have a resurrection body which will be strong and beautiful, similar to Christ's resurrected, glorified body (Rom. 8:11, 23.) Look at Philippians 3:21 and rejoice!

This wonderful process of spiritual renewal has already begun and at Christ's coming will be complete (2 Cor. 3:18; Gal. 4:19; Eph. 4:24).

A glorious certainty (15:53)

There is nothing terminal about death. When a Christian dies the really wonderful journey has only just begun! Read 2 Corinthians 5:2-4. After an interview with Nick Page, David Watson wrote: 'I was amazed by the impact of the broadcast. It was a reminder to me of the enormous interest (and anxiety) about death. It is our one future certainty and there are no answers apart from Christ.'

Christian stewardship (16:1-4)

Paul gives basic teaching about Christian giving in this chapter. The essentials are:

1. Christian concern for those in need (Gal. 2:10; 6:10; 1 John 3:17-18).
2. Regular and systematic giving in proportion to our earnings (16:2). Some tithe – the Old Testament method – but tithing is only the beginning of giving.
3. Giving on the first day of the week, Sunday, the new day for worship, fellowship and commemoration of the resurrection (Rev. 1:10; John 20:1; Acts 20:7). Giving is an act of worship (Phil. 4:18).

David Livingston wrote: 'I will place no value on anything I have or may possess except in relation to the kingdom of Christ. If anything will advance the interests of that kingdom it shall be given away or kept, depending upon which will most promote the glory of Him to whom I owe all my hopes, in time and eternity.'

Let us remember the widow (Luke 21:2-4) who gave two small copper coins – all she had to live on – and Jesus said she had given more than the rich who gave out of their abundance but kept as much or more for themselves.

Guidance (16:5-9)

Paul had, in fact, to change his mind about his return and prolonged visit to Corinth. The issue caused distress both to him and the church and Paul tried to set the Record straight as we read in 2 Corinthians 1:15–2:2.

Open Doors (16:9-12)

'Evangelise to a finish and bring back the king' is an old missionary slogan. Paul's heart burned for mission. The imagery of the open doors is repeated in 2 Corinthians 2:12; Revelation 3:8; Colossians 4:3. There are still such doors of opportunity for the Gospel today.

Paul encouraged the Corinthians to recognise Timothy as his fellow-servant. Paul constantly sought to build him up and defend him (I Cor. 4:17; I Thess. 3:2; Phil. 2:19-24; I Tim. 4:12).

Paul and Apollos were on good terms despite the rivalries existing in Corinth. They were both leaders who had brought many to faith (I Cor. 3:5). It is a small matter who is second as long as Jesus is FIRST!

Final greetings

The Kiss of Peace was a lovely custom of the early church. Later it was not given between men and women. It came to be called 'The Peace'. The church at Corinth needed to be reminded of this!

Maranatha 'Come, O Lord' became a watchword or password in Jerusalem after the persecution of Christians began. It summed up the LIVING HOPE OF CHRIST'S RETURN. Christians would whisper it to each other, often in words their persecutors could not understand.

MARANATHA!

ANSWER GUIDE

The following pages contain an Answer Guide. It is recommended that answers to the questions be attempted before turning to this guide. It is only a guide and the answers given should not be treated as exhaustive.

GUIDE TO INTRODUCTORY STUDY

In this series of studies group members should begin to realise that Christians and churches in the first and twenty-first centuries are much the same! Help the members to understand that Paul's answers and the ways he dealt with the problems so long ago are God's directive for Christians and their fellowships today. Get them to realise that these people mentioned in Acts 18 and I Corinthians were real people, and in the most important aspects of life just like us.

It's a sobering thought that so much of our New Testament, especially 1 and 2 Corinthians and others of Paul's letters were written because of difficulties, problems, mistaken beliefs, sub-Christian behaviour and disorderly worship in the church fellowships! Where would we be without these letters? Make sure your group realise they were real letters!

Most letters were dictated in those days so that the author put his name at the beginning and his signature at the end (see I Cor. 16:21). What a pity they are still often called 'epistles' as if they were not real letters but, of course, 'epistle' is simply the old English word for a 'letter'. Hundreds of letters, written in the first century, have been found preserved in the sands of Egypt. They are from all kinds of people about all sorts of matters. They begin with the name of the sender, 'Robert ...' then the name of the recipient, next a thanksgiving and often a prayer. These were not Christian letters so the prayer was to some false god. The name of the sender was repeated at the end.

If you examine Paul's letters in the New Testament you will see that nearly all of them follow this pattern. They are not careful, academic products written in the seclusion of a study; they are living torrents of words straight from Paul's heart to the heart of the friends to whom he wrote them. In this instance, however, he does base his letter on the issues they had raised with him by sending visitors and a letter.

Perhaps you could discuss with your group some Christian men and women who today are 'missionaries' living in the way Paul lived – earning their living at a secular job as doctors, teachers, nurses, engineers, agriculturalists, etc., yet spreading the Gospel by personal witness, literature and other means. There are many lands where this is the only way westerners can witness as servants of Christ. A friend of the writer flies planes for a commercial airline in Papua New Guinea and so supports himself in pastoring a church.

Please note that these studies are based on the New International Version. Other translations are mentioned where helpful.

GUIDE TO STUDY 1

DAY 1   a) God.
b) To the church of God in Corinth.
c) Set apart ('sanctified'); called to be holy ('saints' AV); worship the Lord Jesus Christ.

DAY 2   a) Grace and Peace.
b) To God the Father and the Lord Jesus Christ.
c) Grace is described as 'undeserved favour'. The Greek word CHARIS carries the idea of a gift and a gift is never earned nor given as a reward. In the language of the Old Testament Hebrew, the parallel word is 'Hesed' and carries the meaning of God's mercy and kindness. Lamentations 3:22 is a good example. When 'grace' is used in reference to humans it suggests 'covenant love' and 'loyalty' (see Hos. 6:6).

DAY 3   a) Grace.
Rich or enriched.
b) It obviously had been heard, received, believed, obeyed, and passed on.

DAY 4   a) God is faithful.
b) Keep them firm, strong, steadfast to the end.
c) So that they would be blameless when Christ came again.

DAY 5   a) There were now divisions, quarrels and a party spirit in the church (sadly it happens today, too).
b) Through Chloe.
c) Paul, Apollos, Peter and Christ. (Find out more about Apollos in Acts 18:24-28.)

DAY 6   a) Preach the Gospel, the Good News about Jesus.
b) In a way that would exalt Christ (and not Paul).

DAY 7   a) Some saw it as foolishness; others (believers) saw it as God's power. (Which is it for you?)
b) Bring people to a knowledge of God (See Acts 17:27; this is all that human wisdom can do.)
c) Christ and Him crucified (I Cor. 1:23; Phil. 1:21).
Personal. Paul emphasises that salvation only comes through this message.

1 CORINTHIANS • ANSWER GUIDE • · · · · ·

GUIDE TO STUDY 2

DAY 1
a) Most were ordinary folk with little claim to fame, education or prestige. Paul says, 'not many ...' and not 'not any ...' so that, presumably, there were a few who, like himself, had a good background.
b) God chose them (v. 27) to be united to Christ (v. 30).
c) Salvation is God's gift; God unites us to Christ.

DAY 2
a) Christ and Him crucified (v. 2).
Converts whose faith rested in God alone (v. 5).
b) Paul relied on the Spirit's enabling.
(We, too, can be strong to witness, in Him.)

DAY 3
a) Approximately six times (can vary with version).
b) By revelation through the Spirit of God.
c) Personal. Jesus promised the Spirit would guide us into the truth.

DAY 4
a) Those without the Spirit (v. 14); the spiritual (v. 15); the 'worldly' (v. 3). They were 'worldly' because of their jealousy and quarrelling.
b) The Word of God to nourish Christians and enable them to grow (mature).

DAY 5
a) Teamwork. God blesses the planting and watering of the seed.
b) 'We are only God's co-workers. You are God's garden, not ours'.
Both of these terms should apply to His children.

DAY 6
a) The one sure foundation – Jesus Christ.
b) One day the fire of God's judgment will test our work. The result will be either reward or loss. (Note that God's work of salvation still stands (3:15) even if our works fail.)

DAY 7
a) As God's temple (His dwelling place).
b) By allowing strife and division to come in.
c) Because God has given us everything we need – we belong to Christ and He belongs to God – the ruler of the universe (see vv. 21-23 in the Living Bible).

GUIDE TO STUDY 3

DAY 1
a) God's 'things'.
b) That they be faithful.
The Lord. (See Heb. 3:2 for two who met this requirement.)

DAY 2
a) Brothers.
b) God.
c) God has given us everything we have. (If we really believe this we should be acting on Matt. 10:8.)

DAY 3
a) As kings, having everything!
b) At the end of the procession, in the last place.
c) Weakness, dishonour, hunger, thirst, poor clothing, beatings, homelessness, hard work, cursings, persecution, insults.
(Point out our responsibility to pray for those who suffer for Christ's sake.)

DAY 4
a) As his 'dear children'. As a spiritual father he had brought them the Good News and to faith in Christ.
b) To remind them of Paul's example and teaching.
c) To use discipline ('whip') or gentleness ('love').

DAY 5
a) Sorrowful.
b) They should have debarred him from the assembly. Such discipline should result in repentance and a renewed relationship with the Lord.

DAY 6
a) Like yeast or leaven spreading through dough.
b) The Lamb of God.
c) Sin. (Draw attention to Exod. 12 especially v. 15.)

DAY 7
a) Not to associate with immoral people.
They were not to associate with immoral people who were claiming to be Christians; immoral people were not allowed to be church members.
b) God.
c) We are to expel those guilty of it from membership.

GUIDE TO STUDY 4

DAY 1
a) They were bringing their disputes before the civil judges. One of the functions of the temple was to serve as a court of law.
They should aim to find wise members of the Christian fellowship to help settle their dispute. He also suggested they should not always try to defend themselves.
b) They had been washed (spiritual regeneration and cleansing), sanctified (set apart for God) and justified (just as if I'd never sinned = made righteous in Christ.)

DAY 2
a) He warned that not everything was beneficial (even though that was the popular morality of the business world of that day) and that there was the danger of becoming enslaved to things we love more than Christ.
b) The fact that he or she is a member of Christ.
c) The resurrection of the body.

DAY 3
a) As a temple (the dwelling place) of the Holy Spirit.
b) We were purchased with the precious lifeblood of the Lamb of God.

DAY 4
a) Each person should have her/his own spouse; each partner should satisfy the other's needs (Heb. 13:4).
b) To spend more time with the Lord.
c) As a gift from God.

DAY 5
a) To marry if they feel they should.
b) No. Point out the Lord's command in Mark 10:11-12 and yet remember that Paul is 'not writing a systematic treatise on divorce. He is answering specific questions' (Tyndale).

DAY 6
a) A Christian man must not divorce his non-Christian wife, nor should a Christian wife divorce her unbelieving husband if he is willing to continue the marriage. (Note that the above instructions apply only when a spouse is converted after marriage.)
The non-Christian spouse might become a Christian.
b) The children are said to be holy.

DAY 7
a) Just where God has placed him/her and in a way that glorifies God.
A converted slave, if offered release, could choose freedom.
c) Christ's. (V. 22 makes this clear. Paul calls himself a bond-slave, e.g. Rom. 1:1.)

GUIDE TO STUDY 5

DAY 1
a) For them to remain as they were (vv. 24, 27, 29, 30, etc.).
b) To please his/her partner (vv. 33-34).
Both husband and wife are to be Christians (v. 39; 2 Cor. 6:14-15).

DAY 2
a) The popular saying of the day was "All possess knowledge" or "Don't try to tell me what to do!". Human knowledge puffs us up (makes us proud); the person who truly loves God is open to God's knowledge (which gives spiritual growth). (See Gal. 4:8-9 and I John 4:7-8.)
b) Idols are lifeless and useless; God is unique, the Creator and Father.
c) As unique, Lord and Christ, the Creator, the reason for our existence.

DAY 3
a) Weak Christians who were unconvinced that idols were dead would imagine that eating this kind of food involved participation in idolatry (vv. 6-7).
b) Personal; example: 'By God's grace I will not act or participate in anything that will weaken a fellow Christian's faith.'

DAY 4
a) That he had planted churches, including that at Corinth. They are the seal of his apostleship. Some say that it is essential to have seen the Lord. However, that is one of four questions that Paul asks the church concerning himself.
b) To be given support and to have a companion with him on his journeys.
c) Soldier, farmer, shepherd.

DAY 5
a) The working ox was to be left unmuzzled so it could eat as it worked.
b) They are to expect a share of the crop.
c) He has sown spiritual (eternal) seed in their souls, so surely they owe something in return.

DAY 6
a) Personal; example: Those who devote themselves wholly to God's work should expect to be cared for by those whom they serve. (See God's instructions for the priests who were totally involved in the service of the Tabernacle Lev. 2:3; 10:13; Num. 3:48; 5:9; 18:9, 12, 21; Deut. 18:3; 2 Kgs. 12:16.)
b) To preach the Gospel.
c) Nothing!

DAY 7
a) To win as many as possible to Christ. Personal.
b) He tried to identify as closely as possible with each group so as to win them for Christ.
c) The law of Christ (v. 21).

1 CORINTHIANS · ANSWER GUIDE · · · · · · · ·

GUIDE TO STUDY 6

DAY 1 a) He or she submits to discipline and rigorous training.
b) To prevent disqualification from the prize in the Christian race.

DAY 2 a) Protected by the cloud; passed through the sea; baptised as followers of Moses; had bread and water (classed as spiritual no doubt due to its special provision).
b) God was not pleased with them.
If you have time, try to find five examples of Israel's failure in Numbers 11:4 6; Exodus 32:6; Numbers 25:1-3; 21:4-9. Suggest to your group members that they think about all the privileges they enjoy. Is our response one of gratitude, obedient service, trust in God's faithfulness or is it more like that of Israel?

DAY 3 a) Practise idolatry, commit sexual immorality; put God to the test; complain.
b) As a warning for us.
c) Everyone has these tests and God in His faithfulness will never allow us to be tempted beyond our ability to bear them, giving us strength to endure. How about encouraging the group to memorise verse 13?

DAY 4 a) The worship of idols.
b) They are said to participate in the blood and body of Christ. (Note that Paul does not say how this happens. It is a spiritual participation and takes place by faith.)

DAY 5 a) To eat a share of the sacrifices offered.
b) To demons.
c) He or she could come under the influence of evil spirits.

DAY 6 a) The interests of others.
b) Not to ask questions about where the meat came from.
c) Same answer as above. Maybe you can suggest modern-day equivalents of "meat offered to idols".
d) If the Christian is told the meat has been offered to idols.
Have the group read chapter 10, verse 33 in several translations and encourage them to memorise it. This should be a priority in our Christian living.

DAY 7 a) Because they were following Paul's teaching (Col. 1:28-29).
b) Men's heads uncovered and women's heads covered.
c) To acknowledge the custom common to all the churches.

GUIDE TO STUDY 7

DAY 1
a) They did more harm than good.
b) Disunity and selfishness. Hunger for some; drunkenness for others.
c) Shaming God's church and embarrassing the poor.

DAY 2
a) From the Lord Himself.
b) Christ's sacrifice for us and God's new covenant or agreement with us (vv. 24-25).
c) Until Jesus comes again.

DAY 3
a) Examine themselves lest they bring judgment on themselves.
b) Physical illness, death (v. 30).
c) By eating to satisfy hunger at home and by waiting for one another.

DAY 4
a) Spiritual gifts (the special abilities the Holy Spirit gives to each Christian).
b) They had worshipped lifeless idols.
c) By what they said about the Lord Jesus: those genuine would emphasise His Lordship and would not curse Him.

DAY 5
a) The church as a whole should benefit (each Christian would have spiritual input into it).
b) In wise counsel, giving knowledge, faith, healing gifts, miracles, ability to speak God's Word, to discern the gifts of the Spirit; tongues and interpretation of tongues.
c) The Holy Spirit gives to each Christian as He wills. Discuss with the group: 'Do we need the "gentle prodding" Paul gives to Timothy?' (2 Tim. 1:6)

DAY 6
a) Some were Jews, some Gentiles; some were slaves and some free.
b) The Holy Spirit.
c) God has made it like this (v. 18; Ps. 139:13-16). He has made it to function very well.

DAY 7
a) Personal; example: each has many different kinds of members but all are necessary.
b) All the parts suffer.
c) Christ's Body.

GUIDE TO STUDY 8

DAY 1   a) No! Paul referred to a 'WAY', the way of love.
b) Eloquence, knowledge, faith, giving, martyrdom.
c) Personal.

DAY 2   a) Patient, kind. Love is not envious, boastful, proud, rude, self-seeking, irritable, mindful of past failures, happy with evil. (Answers will vary slightly according to which translation you use.)
Love protects, trusts, hopes, perseveres.
b) Personal.

DAY 3   a) Love.
b) Prophecies, tongues, knowledge.
c) Faith, hope and love.
Love.

DAY 4   a) Prophecy (proclaiming God's message) and speaking in tongues.
b) Only himself.
c) The whole church.

DAY 5   a) To speak words which can be understood by all.
b) To see it built up.
c) When we pray in an ordinary language.

DAY 6   a) Speak words that can be understood even though they may be few.
b) They would think they were mad.
c) Convicted of sin, judged, secret thoughts revealed; worship God; acknowledge the presence of God among His people.

DAY 7   a) A hymn; teaching; a revelation from God; a message in tongues; an interpretation.
Be of help to the church, i.e. to the Christians.
b) It should not take place.
Everyone – but only one at a time!

GUIDE TO STUDY 9

DAY 1   a) They were to be quiet and not chatter.
b) He wrote what God had commanded him (v. 37).
c) In a proper orderly way.

DAY 2   a) It is to be preached; when received and believed it saves.
b) As the death, burial and resurrection of Jesus Christ.
That Christ died for our sins.
c) The Scriptures had prophesied it; Peter, the Twelve, five hundred disciples, James, all the apostles and even Paul had seen Him. Matthew 28:16-17; Luke 24:34; John 20:19; Acts 1:2-8 back up these statements in Corinthians.

DAY 3   a) As an encounter with the Lord and a receiving of God's grace.
b) Because he had persecuted God's church.
c) Personal.

DAY 4   a) That the dead would not be raised. The resurrection of Christ proves this statement false.
b) Preaching and believing in God would be meaningless. Faith is a delusion. We are still in our sins. Believers who have died are lost eternally.

DAY 5   a) The resurrection of all who put their trust in Him.
b) Through the man Christ Jesus.
c) When Christ comes again.
d) Death.

DAY 6   a) As literally a daily dying.
b) He was convinced of the resurrection of Jesus Christ (and hence the truthfulness of the Gospel message); he was acting not from 'human reasons' (v. 32).

DAY 7   a) How will it happen, what will our resurrection bodies be like?
b) To sowing seeds in the ground in order for new plants to grow.
c) Angels have their own beauty and glory; the sun, moon and stars have varying degrees of brilliance – in the same way our resurrection bodies will be supernatural, spiritual and glorious (vv. 39-44).

GUIDE TO STUDY 10

DAY 1   a) Before: mortal, ugly, weak, physical. After: immortal, beautiful, strong, spiritual.
b) As a life-giving Spirit.
c) The likeness of Jesus, the 'man from heaven' (v. 49).
d) To share in God's kingdom.

DAY 2   a) We will ALL be changed.
b) Victory through our Lord Jesus Christ.
c) Their work for the Lord.
d) It is never useless, never in vain.

DAY 3   a) It should be regular, planned and in proportion to our income. Those who handle such gifts should be trustworthy.

DAY 4   a) Macedonia.
b) He didn't want a short visit and any visit would be as the Lord opened the way for it.
c) There were great opportunities for service.

DAY 5   a) They were to make him feel welcome as he was working for the Lord.
b) Brother.
c) Visit the Christians at Corinth.

DAY 6   a) Be on guard; stand firm; be courageous; be strong; do everything in love.
b) As being the first Christians in Achaia and serving God's people.
c) Cheered Paul up.

DAY 7   a) Churches in Asia, Aquila and Priscilla, and the church that met in their home.
b) With a holy kiss.
c) Those who do not love the Lord.
d) 'The Grace' i.e. that the love and favour of God should rest upon them.

THE WORD WORLDWIDE

We first heard of WORD WORLDWIDE over twenty years ago when Marie Dinnen, its founder, shared excitedly about the wonderful way ministry to one needy woman had exploded to touch many lives. It was great to see the Word of God being made central in the lives of thousands of men and women, then to witness the life-changing results of them applying the Word to their circumstances. Over the years the vision for WORD WORLDWIDE has not dimmed in the hearts of those who are involved in this ministry. God is still at work through His Word and in today's self-seeking society, the Word is even more relevant to those who desire true meaning and purpose in life. WORD WORLDWIDE is a ministry of WEC International, an interdenominational missionary society, whose sole purpose is to see Christ known, loved and worshipped by all, particularly those who have yet to hear of His wonderful name. This ministry is a vital part of our work and we warmly recommend the WORD WORLDWIDE 'Geared for Growth' Bible studies to you. We know that as you study His Word you will be enriched in your personal walk with Christ. It is our hope that as you are blessed through these studies, you will find opportunities to help others discover a personal relationship with Jesus. As a mission we would encourage you to work with us to make Christ known to the ends of the earth.

Stewart and Jean Moulds – British Directors, **WEC International**.

A full list of over 50 'Geared for Growth' studies can be obtained from:

John and Ann Edwards
5 Louvaine Terrace, Hetton-le-Hole, Tyne & Wear, DH5 9PP
Tel. 0191 5262803 Email: rhysjohn.edwards@virgin.net

Anne Jenkins
2 Windermere Road, Carnforth, Lancs., LA5 9AR
Tel. 01524 734797 Email: anne@jenkins.abelgratis.com

UK Website: www.gearedforgrowth.co.uk

Christian Focus Publications

publishes books for all ages

Our mission statement –

STAYING FAITHFUL

In dependence upon God we seek to help make His infallible word, the Bible, relevant. Our aim is to ensure that the Lord Jesus Christ is presented as the only hope to obtain forgiveness of sin, live a useful life and look forward to heaven with Him.

REACHING OUT

Christ's last command requires us to reach out to our world with His gospel. We seek to help fulfil that by publishing books that point people towards Jesus and help them develop a Christ-like maturity. We aim to equip all levels of readers for life, work, ministry and mission.

Books in our adult range are published in three imprints.

Christian Focus contains popular works including biographies, commentaries, basic doctrine, and Christian living. Our children's books are also published in this imprint.

Mentor focuses on books written at a level suitable for Bible College and seminary students, pastors, and other serious readers; the imprint includes commentaries, doctrinal studies, examination of current issues, and church history.

Christian Heritage contains classic writings from the past.

For details of our titles visit us on our website
www.christianfocus.com

Christian Focus Publications Ltd
Geanies House, Fearn, Tain,
Ross-shire, IV20 ITW, Scotland, United Kingdom.
info@christianfocus.com